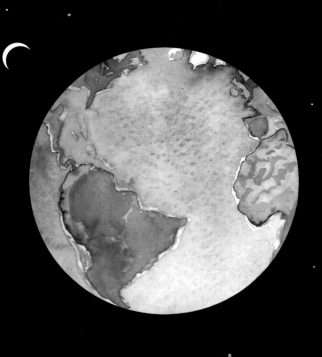

For the planet —J.C.

For my favorite nature advocates: Noah, Vallen, and Hero —N.C.

If We Were Gone

Imagining the World without People

John Coy

illustrations by
Natalie Capannelli

Millbrook Press
Minneapolis

People need water to live.

We need air to breathe.

We need plants to survive.

But do they need us?

Maybe not.

Imagine what would happen
if people were no longer here.

Pipes would burst
and pavement buckle.

With cars and factories stopped,
pollution would decrease.

Plants would spread out
and new trees take root.

Without electricity for pumps, water would flood.

Roofs would leak
and houses and buildings collapse.

Lightning strikes would start fires that would burn uncontrolled.

Around the world,
things would break down—

schools, stadiums, books, computers.

Some materials would last longer— bronze, silver, gold, ceramic.

But bit by bit, year by year,
what humans made
would fade.

Water would find its own level
and carve out new channels.

The air would become cleaner with each rainfall.

Plants and animals would grow wild
and forests and jungles expand.

Does air need us?
No.

Do plants need us?
No.

Does water need us?
No.

Do we need them?

Absolutely.

And because we do,
we must take care,
in all the ways we can,

TRAILHEAD

so we're here on Earth together
now
and in the future.

Author's Note

As a boy, I traveled to forty-nine states with my family. My father loved to drive and took us to mountains, forests, prairies, deserts, lakes, rivers, and oceans. He enjoyed being outside, observing closely, and spotting animals and birds. From him, I developed my sense of wonder for the natural world.

I grew up in Wisconsin, where Gaylord Nelson was one of our senators. On April 22, 1970, he helped establish Earth Day to raise awareness about the damage we were doing to our planet and to learn about better ways to take care of our air, water, and plants. I still have my button from that day.

Years later, as an adult, I read Alan Wiseman's fascinating book *The World without Us* about what would happen if people were no longer here. That book had a big impact on how I looked at things I'd always been intrigued by: abandoned houses, farms, and buildings. Such places brought up so many questions. Who lived here? Where did they go? Why did they leave? I also was struck by how quickly the plants and trees reclaimed the landscape after humans left.

The idea for *If We Were Gone* was sparked by a conversation with the poet Juliet Patterson. We were talking about climate change and the environment and what would happen to the world if people were no longer on Earth. The next day, I started working on the story. It made its way to my editor, Carol Hinz, and she embraced it and has helped make it better every step of the way. I'm also grateful to Natalie Capannelli for her stunning illustrations and Danielle Carnito for her excellent art direction. Special thanks to Adam Lerner, Lindsay Matvick, Libby Stille, and everybody at Lerner Publishing Group for all that they do.

While I was working on *If We Were Gone*, I took a trip with my friend Gary Cerkvenik to the Boundary Waters Canoe Area Wilderness on the border of northern Minnesota and Ontario, Canada. We hiked in on the same two-mile portage we had been on thirty-nine years earlier. There's plenty of time to think on a portage that long, and as I breathed in the clean air, I paid attention to the water and plants we passed. I looked closely and noted changes where a small section of a lake had filled in. But overall, the granite rocks, the clear water, and the variety of trees were remarkably the same.

When we reached the end of the portage, we put the canoe in the water, set the packs in, and began paddling on Angleworm Lake. As I looked around, I had the clear realization that this wilderness area didn't need us at all. It would be just fine without us. And so it is with the planet. It does not need us. We need it.

What Can We Do?

"Virtually 99.999 percent of all life on the planet has gone extinct," says Hans-Dieter Sues, curator of vertebrate paleontology at the Smithsonian Institution's National Museum of Natural History. No matter what we think, human beings are not exempt from this. If we do not make significant changes in how we live, we will meet this same fate.

What can we do? Acknowledging the problem is a big first step. Unfortunately, many adults are reluctant to admit that we have significant problems in taking care of our air, water, plants, and planet.

Think about the many decisions you make each day. What do you buy? Where does it come from? How is it made? What do you reuse, recycle, or throw away? These individual decisions add up and have a substantial impact on life on the planet.

One important thing to do is to make a point of spending more time outside. Find a spot you like and sit down and take a deep breath. Look closely at the plants you see. Pay attention to any insects. Listen for sounds of birds and animals. Spending more time outside will change the way you see the world.

Like many changes, developing a new relationship with our air, water, plants, and animals is going to be led by young people. Many of them have already taken leadership roles in asking questions, studying these challenges, and offering solutions.

This is the planet you are going to live on. What will you do to protect it? What will you do to learn more? What will you do so that humans can continue to live here for generations to come?

Selected Bibliography

Kolbert, Elizabeth. *The Sixth Extinction: An Unnatural History.* New York: Henry Holt, 2014.

Leslie, John. *The End of the World: The Science and Ethics of Human Extinction.* London: Routledge, 1996.

Stafford, William. *The Way It Is: New & Selected Poems.* St. Paul: Graywolf Press, 1998.

Tennesen, Michael. *The Next Species: The Future of Evolution in the Aftermath of Man.* New York: Simon & Schuster, 2015.

Wallace-Wells, David. *The Uninhabitable Earth: Life after Warming.* New York: Tim Duggan Books, 2019.

Weisman, Alan. *The World without Us.* New York: Thomas Dunne Books, 2007.

Wilson, Edward O. *The Future of Life.* New York: Alfred A. Knopf, 2002.

Zalasiewicz, Jan. *The Earth after Us: What Legacy Will Humans Leave in the Rocks?* Oxford: Oxford University Press, 2008.

Millbrook Press™
An imprint of Lerner Publishing Group, Inc.
241 First Avenue North
Minneapolis, MN 55401 USA

For reading levels and more information, look up this title at www.lernerbooks.com.

Original Earth Day button courtesy John Coy, p. 30.
Designed by Danielle Carnito.
Main body text set in Mikado Medium. Typeface provided by HVD Fonts.
The illustrations in this book were created with watercolor, digital techniques, and tiny brushes.

Acknowledgment: Special thanks to Dr. Jeffrey J. Clark, Professor of Geology, Lawrence University, for reviewing the text and illustrations for accuracy.

Library of Congress Cataloging-in-Publication Data

Names: Coy, John, 1958– author. | Capannelli, Natalie, 1980– illustrator.
Title: If we were gone : imagining the world without people / John Coy ; illustrated by Natalie Capannelli.
Description: Minneapolis, MN, USA : Millbrook Press, [2020] | Audience: Age 7–11. | Audience: K to grade 3.
Identifiers: LCCN 2019001065 (print) | LCCN 2019012967 (ebook) | ISBN 9781541578920 (eb pdf) | ISBN 9781541523579 (lb : alk. paper)
Subjects: LCSH: Human ecology—Juvenile literature. | Nature—Effect of human beings on—Juvenile literature.
Classification: LCC GF48 (ebook) | LCC GF48 .C69 2020 (print) | DDC 304.2—dc23

LC record available at https://lccn.loc.gov/2019001065

Manufactured in the United States of America
1-44484-34693-8/6/2019